GODDESS

GODDESS

Cheryl Tan

QUERENCIA

Querencia Press – Chicago IL

ISBN 978 1 963943 99 3

.

www.querenciapress.com

First Published in 2024

Querencia Press, LLC
Chicago IL

Printed & Bound in the United States of America

For Thazin.

CONTENTS

holy

and i stole you the way a child steals candy from the temple
glucose gems on a red glass plate. you, oh utmost charity
you were the bell i tossed coins at, below the fountain of guan yin
the water i bathed the buddha with, the candle that wouldn't
go out. you, oh sweet veneration, fresh jasmine on gold

reprieve

standing back to back   we spin around we lie
seraphs with six wings
                        spirits of the air
                                 raindrop eyes
                                        mantra chime
bells at their feet
draw a circle and dance around it
birds folded like talismans—birds kissing like
tears baptism of the earth and its manic woes

                            oh my goddess   i've finally met you
                          karma mirrored into eternity infinity
              the earth turns around   bringing you and me with it
all things turn around   yes   all things turn around
hoc est corpus meum   extend your hands
in submission and i will sing a song about
how we   born blind   are still   we repeat
taking our little lives   we extend them   we pray

it was nice to meet you.
it was nice to be here.

Fragments

The first pictograph spells
亻, the radical for human,
drawn upright
as though pierced by ink.
Three strokes more &
it spells 代, which means to
substitute.

To replace one pound of
flesh with another, graft a
language onto foreign
tongue.
Can you do it?

Can you take the pieces of a
country & meld them,
pilgrims on the shore?
Your bubbly native script
marrying
sharp chalk & stone
The second half of your
name spells 欣,
brushed slowly over foolscap
like an anguished cry, a
revelation of tomorrow -

Let my words sing with
your words.

honorary hollowscape

1.   the matchstick

can you count down to the moments when memory turns
diegetic, the forcing of marrow out of bone, ash
out of body? can you hiccup fingers, grow new toes
amber eyes, smouldering tones
combustible hearts   digested glass shards
          amidst a pile of gremlin faces
they say to be gullible is to break
to waver, haze past the ocean
a whistle - gelatinous thistle. fermented daisy
          living the life of watered bliss, rainpaint world
a madwoman's kiss

2.   the fire

                    will o' the wisp
   broken where you cannot reach, a hole too deep to let light in
a blossom disintegrating against the clock, swallowing gunmetal
          bulleted brain, minused ruination, watered down
clowning around   advertised teeth and questionable gifts. the
sky woven around the night is
a ring around the eyes   you are love's new scratching post
inflamed skin and sunken grooves each stanza out of place
a story retold   an appropriate time   the mind's personal bonfire
cyclical jellyfish of humanity. biscuit tin metafiction,
streetwise failings. child of the world but there is none and
you are just sorrowful sorrow

you flew with her over the country there was a pyre you
fell into   wandering ribs amidst blooming weeds.
obfuscated vegetation

3.   *the magic*

    when she knows what you know without
knowing the knowledge of knowing and you are flickering and
fluttering in fluttery flickering delight night bright keep me
    shining bright tonight. your little demon playground
you want not words but the blind remnants of them
    a language where my mind is a dustbin, a coke can
within a fist. an eviscerated tendon
    with lipstick bloodied hanging

Goddess

Goddess in the flesh, goddess of my heart. Open yourself in the light of dawn, put on a red jacket and make breakfast with me. Is it selfish that I can see you and me like this? Two old people breathing and alive, with apricot faces, ambrosia smiles?

Senseless noise, domestic nonsense. In the wake of my humanness I weep, my hands on the floor, my forehead at your feet. I am afraid. Afraid of loving. Afraid of growing up, afraid of growing old. The stench of my fears is distinctly mortal; they decay with each passing moment. Every day I drown in a dream I cannot wake from, and at the end of every heaven I see you.

Perhaps in some foreign universe we could have been equals. Last night you were rain and I was famine, and you came when I cried out for you. Your words caught fire down my back, your smile was oil upon a clay altar. *Mea culpa. Mea culpa. Mea maxima culpa.* Intimacy is a fountain that I drink from, your chest a hollow crevice where I yield.

Lovely loneliness, lonely loveliness. When you linger, angels sing from above. When you leave, the stars leave with you. Goddess in the flesh, goddess of my heart, you open yourself in the light of my fears and yet I still have so many. I fear sacrificing myself to the spectre of you, the last mirage of a man dying of thirst. The moment I finally decide to love, only for you to decide you no longer loved me.

All I ask is to be let in, to lie down in your arms like blood lapping at a heart. I want to bask in the temple of your presence. I want to bear the burden of watching you cry.

Break me. Remake me. Incarnate me. A bed of spider lilies, spirit maiden's atrophy. Is it selfish that I can see you and me like this? A petal's worth of stillness, a tsunami's worth of rain. I want you to come down from your lotus and live on earth with me. I want to hold to you the illusion of forever.

Armenian Church, Singapore

The heat of the day, the whitened effigies, the dead man's garden, the voyeur in me peeling back dirt. Stepping on your father's generations removed. Adjacent the church with its box of donations. Two dollars per postcard. Photographer Christopher Tan. Under a fan I attempt to pray. Nothing. Distant yammerings of resurrection. To some extent we are descended from angels, doomed to the soil beneath our feet. I pay the two dollars. Can we take a picture? No, no, of course not. Shove me in a cupboard if you have to, just don't let me die alone.

Padma

When I was young I used to lie on my grand-aunt's mattress and listen to sutras on the radio. Long droning warbles out of a black plastic box, chants in sanskrit that I could not place consonants to. Chants like scarabs, like grandparents' hands, the ghost of sounds called to lull you to sleep. Drooling on a pillow amidst the marbled floor, holding compact discs up to the light. A child's refracted psychedelia. In my sleep faceless bodhisattvas beckoned me.

I suppose I was raised religious. The jewel is in the lotus. The virtues of compassion. Even then I would dream of someone to take me away, to breathe out and anoint me as beloved. To recollect the pieces and compress them in a hue of golden light, hold me beneath the cold unyielding sky. As an atheist divinity comes to me in the little things: the dark aureole of a slow heated night, the warmth of your hand dancing in mine.

Padma, padma, pure flower of the mud. This is the way I commemorate you.

sans merci

Strange as it was, the way you laughed when I told you I once
ogled you from afar - when you said you weren't anything to look
at. I've been up for days over days undulating
bows in my hair - cloth over my eyes - gouging them out
biblical-style - quasi pillowcase trauma where I
stuffed this poem where you were undying and I was untrying -
where I cracked my face on your sofa and you fixed my
tattered nose - scattered behind the curtains - You broke my face
on your shoulder and I said thank you - thank you - to your voice
over the telephone - the day you used me to
sweep your house

       A certain worthless kind of confession - scratched on the
borders of a Singaporean sea - checkpoint with no light - from
Sengkang to Clementi

       To cup with fingers a nose red and round, from weeping
or worse - the circus of dreams hanged & forgotten
Trapezing the hazed summer heat - strange as it is without the red
of your frock - or the fact I have one just like it - two weddings
dressed in blood - unsullied and unpolished
When people knelt before empty beds - niches abandoned and
yearning - deserted without titles
The exiled living in the xenophobic night - peeling or skidding? -
shrieking or pulling? C'est la vie - yes - but how can I look back
and live under the same secret street - the old clandestine prayer -
the old trick in the book

Where we walked this road like it was ours - a pilgrim's conquered state - Thighs - breasts - brown as earth & equally ploughed - alone and palely loitering. Fey children among the meads - guilty as sin - to cup with fingers a trembling face - to pin down the soul and display it. You made garlands out of paper and crowned us - pillow princess to the end - we lay on the couch and you dabbed lipstick on my neck as I cried - you said you would take care of me.

kaddish

the present is as flawless as you make it. you
look up from the floor at the tin of cooling powder
lavender scented, bellflowers on the label. rosemary,
geranium, eucalyptus, patchouli. incense steaming
through an air purifier. over time you have
learned to recall aftertastes
xanax bitter. zyprexa sweet.

her voice wet ash on flowers.
she takes your hands and blows on them, and you realise
they are cold. talk to me, honey, won't you talk to me?
her hair hangs in sheets down her collar. there was this girl
she says, in the ambulance. her heart stopped beating
halfway. can you forgive me for her?

outside the rain comes like a baptism, like penance

Requiem

There was a time when everything moved slow, like a kind of forgetting, the kind of sobriety gained after loss. You have me right where you'd like me, darling, but I can't do it anymore. Somewhere along the hillside I stop heeding your call, stop turning my head to face you.

In my head, you were a much better person. In my head, I cared for you properly. Gorge on loss, why not, because you are air and I a chord around my neck and so many things I keep from you in fear of terrifying you.

It seems like a dream.

I thought I knew what was good for me and I thought I wouldn't lose it

Proto-heartbreak to a language I spoke before I met you. The lexicons of loss. The axioms of love and their corresponding rituals. It's so laughable that I could cry, that sick lull of forever, and everywhere I look I find another goodbye. Craziest of crazies, the moon rises and I fall free far away from sleep

Maybe the next time we meet it will be war and I would be fighting with my words and you would be fighting to keep my flesh on me. Guts and ink, baby. Guts and ink. Years ago someone called me brother. Years ago I turned into a woman.

I remember the day we dressed for each other. You borrowed your mother's jumpsuit and I wore handmade jewelery, and walked in the rain under one umbrella. I remember the raffia ribbon you tied around your wrist to call you mine. I remember coming to your house to bake gingerbread, the way your eyes trained themselves on the icing. So many things laid out on an altar. So many things I try to forget.

The details of the crash went like this. Two steps into oncoming traffic, my ribs beneath an impending wheel. I buckle mid-scream, tremble mid-groan, each cry an open street back to where you were, where I was, where we were. I loved and I loved and I am left twitching on my back, frothing, limbs flailing at the sky. Tables. Chairs. Moans of despair. The naked shadow of you exposed and fleeting. I open my mouth, I knock on a door, as though my answer would cause the house to fall.

I sit by your bed picking up my possessions. We comfort people with words we wish to hear.

ai ai ai the flowers have opened. ai ai ai the sun has set. Dream where I woke up with you and your bed head looked pretty. Dream in which I consumed you whole. Maybe being 16 is the nightmare, where you fall in love with every smile you see, bruise yourself on every corner of the room. I am so clumsy in this universe of sorrows, in this primordial earth of pain.

To find happiness amidst tears and fears, as well as you –

www.ingramcontent.com/pod-product-compliance
Lightning Source LLC
Chambersburg PA
CBHW061330120626
46546CB00007B/2743